D1713612

How to Play Dizi for Beginners

The Ultimate Guide to Learning, Playing, and Becoming Proficient at the Instrument

© **Copyright 2023 - All rights reserved.**

The content contained within this book may not be reproduced, duplicated, or transmitted without direct written permission from the author or the publisher.

Under no circumstances will any blame or legal responsibility be held against the publisher, or author, for any damages, reparation, or monetary loss due to the information contained within this book, either directly or indirectly.

<u>Legal Notice:</u>

This book is copyright protected. It is only for personal use. You cannot amend, distribute, sell, use, quote, or paraphrase any part of the content within this book without the consent of the author or publisher.

<u>Disclaimer Notice:</u>

Please note the information contained within this document is for educational and entertainment purposes only. All effort has been executed to present accurate, up-to-date, reliable, and complete information. No warranties of any kind are declared or implied. Readers acknowledge that the author is not engaging in the rendering of legal, financial, medical, or professional advice. The content within this book has been derived from various sources. Please consult a licensed professional before attempting any techniques outlined in this book.

By reading this document, the reader agrees that under no circumstances is the author responsible for any losses, direct or indirect, that are incurred as a result of the use of the information contained within this document, including, but not limited to, errors, omissions, or inaccuracies.

Table of Contents

Introduction

Few instruments are as magical as the dizi. It's a simple one with no bells and whistles, and yet the sound you can create with it is nothing short of transcendent. This instrument is rich in history, spanning centuries, and even now, it continues to interest one and all. The dizi has reached out through ancient times to tap you on the shoulder and demand your attention, and you have answered its call because you are a musician at heart.

As you go through the pages of this in-depth guide, you will learn about the rich history of the dizi. You'll discover how it became what it is today. Whether you're a musician with some skill already or only starting out with the dizi, you'll be glad you chose this book out of all the others. It does away with confusing theories and terminologies, simplifying things so you can pick up a dizi right away and play notes to your heart's content. Written in simple English, you won't feel lost as you read and learn.

So, as you read this book, allow it to take you by the hand and walk you through the whats and hows of playing this marvelous instrument. You'll soon learn how to balance technical skill and your personal, creative touch while playing this ancient flute. If you're eager and happy to learn this skill, there's not a moment to lose. Head to the first chapter and become acquainted with the dizi.

Chapter 1: Background of the Dizi

So, you want to learn to play the dizi. Who wouldn't? With its delicate, ethereal sound, this lovely instrument has thrilled many ears for years. Something about the dizi tugs at your heart's strings. Part of the power and allure of music is its ability to transport you anywhere. As you listen to the dizi, it paints a picture of worlds you've never been to very vividly, and while you can't describe those realms, you know them in your heart. You long to be there. It feels like home. So, it makes sense that you'd want to learn how to play. So, before getting down to the business of playing the dizi, how about a history lesson? It's only fitting to appreciate the origin and evolution of the instrument you're about to master.

1. *Something about the dizi tugs at your heart's strings. Source: https://unsplash.com/photos/an-open-book-on-a-table-ozUIiFEC8Zg*

The What's, Where's, and When's of the Dizi

"Dizi" is pronounced deed-zuh, with stress on the second syllable. The "zuh" part sounds like the schwa sound, which is like a cross between "uh" and "ah." Still confused? Think about how a British person would pronounce the vowel sound in the second half of the word "doctor," and you have the schwa sound. You're welcome. You were promised a history lesson, not an English lesson, so it's time to talk about the history of this instrument.

This Chinese transverse flute you want to learn to play is a prominent part of Chinese music, whether folk music, opera, or even present-day Chinese orchestral music. Many people in China have this instrument because it's easy to make. It's also portable, so they can take it on the go wherever they want. In a world sorely needing leisure and rest, it's nice to know you can whip out your dizi wherever and have fun since it's not bulky to carry. Usually, this instrument is crafted from bamboo. If you hear someone refer to your dizi as a Chinese bamboo flute, don't assume they're trying to downgrade your instrument. Some people think of the dizi as being part of the woodwind family, but since this instrument is Chinese in origin, it's more accurate to say it's part of the bamboo family of instruments. The koudi, bawu, guanzi, and xiao are also part of this group.

There are different versions of this instrument. If you look at the Northern Chinese version, you'll find it's made of violet or purple bamboo. Check out the Hangzhou and Suzhou versions, and you'll see they're cut from white bamboo instead. Head over to the southern parts of China, like Chaozhou, and the dizi there will likely be made from a lighter-colored bamboo than the others. The southern Chinese dizi is lighter in weight, and when you play it, you'll notice its tone is quieter than the other versions. Sometimes, the dizi is made of different kinds of wood. There are dizis made of stones like jade – a beautiful green, white, or yellow mineral. You're right to assume a jade dizi would be pricier than a bamboo one. Collectors love them because they look beautiful. Some dizi players also enjoy having an instrument that looks as good as the musical pieces they play. Does that mean you should empty your wallet, break your piggy bank, and clear your bank account to get a jade one? No. You can enjoy quality sounds from a bamboo or wooden dizi, so there's no need to lose your shirt trying to buy a jade one.

The transverse flute has existed for over 9,000 years in China, although there was a time when it didn't have the mokong. What's that, you wonder? You'll learn about that in the next chapter. Archeologists have discovered pieces of this flute, which were made of bone. Why bone? Since bones are hollow, it made sense at the time to use them to craft the dizi since there was no need to carve out the central hole. The practice of making all kinds of flutes from bone is ancient... as old as 42,000 years. Remarkably, if you could get your hands on one of the fragments of the transverse flutes, you'd find you can still play it. How cool would that be... playing an instrument from 9,000 years ago? These ancient, simple transverse flutes are stunningly similar to the present-day dizi. Even the hole placements are alike.

The origin of the present version of the dizi has been traced back to the 5th century BC. If you're interested in seeing the dizi's ancestors, you can head to China's central Henan province and check out the Jiahu neolithic site. There, you'll see flutes from 7,000 to 5,000 BC, with five to eight holes. If you could play them, you'd get a range of notes that just about cover an octave, which is the range of notes between one musical note and the next higher version of that same note. If you're old enough to remember the Do Re Mi song from Sound of Music, you know there's a world of difference between the first Do and the final Do.

The Dizi in Traditional and Contemporary Music

Did you know that the dizi used to be called the hengchul? It's true. Hengchul means "horizontal blow." With time, it would be called the hengdi, meaning "horizontal flute," before people would call it the dizi. During the epoch of the Sul and Tang dynasties, music would take an exciting turn as people warmed up to the melodies of flutes and the beating of drums. This made the dizi even more popular and essential in Chinese music. The dizi's prominence grew in musicals, operas, and folk music after the Ching Dynasty. One of the things that cemented the instrument's place in traditional music is its resonance. As part of traditional compositions, it brought the music to life with its distinct timbre that couldn't be replicated by any other instrument.

2. The dizi's prominence grew in musicals, operas, and folk music after the Ching Dynasty. Source: Metropolitan Museum of Art, CC0, via Wikimedia Commons: https://commons.wikimedia.org/wiki/File:Dizi_(%E7%AC%9B%E 5%AD%90_)_MET_89.4.61_slide.jpg

Even now, the dizi remains evocative when used in contemporary music. It is more commonly played in Chinese orchestras. What's brilliant about these orchestras is they have found ways to blend the themes and movements of Western symphony structure with Chinese instruments, which include the dizi. What does this mean? Think about a movie. It has a beginning, a middle, and an end, and all these parts contain a piece of the puzzle of the story being put together. These parts exist in music, too, and they are known as movements. Each movement in a musical piece is a part of the whole musical story. Now, think of your favorite protagonist or main character in any movie. They show up at the beginning, in the middle, and at the end of the story because they matter. Without this character, there would be no story, and no one would care to watch the movie. The same thing happens in music, except that the musical character is called a theme. That's the part of the musical piece that is played repeatedly.

By bringing it all together, the dizi becomes an actor in a play or a movie. When the Chinese orchestras play it, it embodies the themes of the musical piece, helping to tell the story. Sometimes, the dizi will be the star of the show, like when it is played on its own as a solo melody. Other times, it's part of an ensemble cast, played in harmony with other instruments in order to complement them. These orchestras also use Western playing techniques and styles, demonstrating the versatility of the dizi.

Setting Expectations for Beginners

Before you learn to play the dizi, you should know what to expect so you don't feel blindsided. First, know that it will take time and practice to master this instrument. Playing the dizi is a skill unlike any other. No one is born with a skill except virtuosos, who definitely wouldn't need this book. If you feel stuck at any point in your learning journey or are tempted to quit because it seems complicated, remember – all you need is time and consistent practice.

You're reading this book because you want to succeed at playing the dizi, aren't you? Well, if you're going to pull it off, make peace with failure. The attitude you have toward failing will determine your success. You will slow your progress if you beat yourself up for not getting something right. If you hand in the towel because you find an aspect of the dizi challenging, then it has all been for nothing. So, right out of the gate, expect challenges and accept that you won't be good at it right away.

Now that you have the proper mindset to approach your learning journey, what else should you expect? Playing the dizi requires a proper form. You can't put your lips on it and blow however you please and expect that it will do. Your playing will sound terrible. So, expect to master the proper mouth shape for this instrument. Whenever you read or hear embouchure, remember it's a description of the shape of your mouth when playing the dizi or any other wind instrument.

Your playing will also be affected by the dizi's dimo, which you'll learn more about in the next chapter. So, knowing how to attach the dimo to your dizi correctly and making the adjustments is critical. Do this wrong, and your dizi may not have its signature resonant sound. You'll learn how to position your fingers properly and maintain good posture while playing so you don't develop a cramp, and you can carry on as long as you want. Breath control is also a vital thing to have when playing the dizi. You'll get better at using your breath with time, but if you want to have even better control, regular cardio exercises will help with your lung capacity.

Once you have that down, you can play short and easy pieces. After mastering these, you can't stop there, or else you'll plateau. You might even lose interest in the dizi, which isn't the goal. So, what do you do? You move on to more complex pieces. By spending time learning the more straightforward songs, you'll have the confidence to tackle more challenging musical pieces that require intricate playing techniques. You should also practice along with a piano to find the right notes and stay on pitch.

So, you've come to the end of the first chapter. You've discovered the fascinating lore of the dizi and how it holds a place in music, both old and new. You also understand what to expect as you learn to play the dizi. You're just about ready to get started with your dizi in the next chapter. However, something has been held back from you deliberately until this point. Why? It's an uncomfortable truth that, when confronted, it forces a make-or-break decision. Are you ready? Here it goes: There's no point where the learning ends. That's the truth in all its naked glory.

If you assumed that there would be some pinnacle, some point of mastery you hit where you never have to practice or learn anything further, that's not the case. Even the greats make a point of playing every day. Think of your newly-acquired dizi-playing skills as a muscle. You know what they say about muscle: Use it or lose it. Daily practice does more than help you stay sharp with your playing. As you play, you'll discover your personal style, refine it, and pick up on tricks you may not have known about otherwise. There's no "top" when it comes to learning any skill, and playing the dizi is no exception to this rule.

So, this begs the question: What keeps the professionals with years of experience and skill going? What would cause anyone to continue doing something they can now do blindfolded? The answer is a simple one. People who continue to learn are in love with the process. That's it. There's no destination to get to. They may have set goals, like learning to control their breath or pulling off a complex fingering technique. However, in the grand scheme of things, they play the dizi because they love it. Can you accept that your learning journey will take as long as it takes? Can you make peace with knowing there will always be something to learn, even when you're a pro? If you can, then you are more likely to have fun. Having fun means you're in the state of mind to improve rapidly. That's a good thing. If you love being a lifelong learner, you're ready for the next chapter.

Chapter 2: Getting Started with Your Dizi

You're about to immerse yourself in the magic and mystique of the dizi. The people who got it in their heads to invent this instrument deserve monuments in their honor. Why? The dizi's sound is hauntingly beautiful. Each note you play on it is pregnant with the wisdom of ancient times. With your instrument, you can weave melodies that awaken your soul, make the magic feel real, and cause your sleeping neighbor to have dreams of being an Emperor in ancient China.

Before you get that good at playing the dizi, you have some more learning to do. Do you know what a dizi looks like? What about its parts? Will you need all ten fingers to play, or do you need an extra hand? How do you set up your dizi? How do you take care of it? What's the best dizi for you? You're going to discover all this and more in this chapter.

The Dizi's Parts

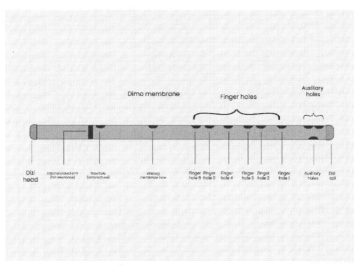

3.   *You're about to immerse yourself in the magic and mystique of the dizi. Source: https://qiangu9461.files.wordpress.com/2013/03/2.png*

The Mouthpiece: This bit is where you blow into the dizi. When you look at it, you'll notice it's crafted to allow the air to flow freely from your mouth into the dizi's body. As mentioned before, you need the proper technique in order to blow correctly. If your embouchure is good, then the sounds you create as you blow into the mouthpiece will also be good. The mouthpiece is fitted on the head joint.

The Body: The dizi's body is usually crafted from bamboo, as you know, except when it isn't. The bamboo material is why the dizi has great tonal resonance, giving it that quality that causes people to connect with their deeper selves. The dizi's pitch depends on the body's width (or diameter). How does this work? The broader and longer your instrument is, the lower the pitches you'll create as you play.

Conversely, the narrower and shorter it is, the higher the notes you play will sound.

The Finger Holes: The finger holes are precisely what you suspect them to be. They're holes you cover with your fingers in order to play various notes. By covering some holes and leaving others open, you vary the pitch of the music. How? You're affecting where the air flows through the dizi's body and how much air stays in it. As you change the quantity of vibrating air in the body, the note's pitch changes.

The Mokong: This hole is an extra hole between the finger holes and the mouthpiece of your dizi. You can't play your dizi without it. Otherwise, it wouldn't be a dizi anymore.

The Dimo: Look at a dizi if you have one, and you will notice a membrane that keeps the mokong covered. This membrane is the dimo. When you play, you'll notice the dimo vibrating. This vibration is what lends to the resonance of the dizi. You can adjust the dimo however you want in order to change the quality of the sound. It is usually made of cattail reed... far thinner than paper.

Assembling and Caring for Your Dizi

The following are the steps you should follow to assemble your dizi if it didn't come preassembled:

1. First, take the head and fix it onto the body. Check to ensure the hole you blow through lines up correctly with the first finger hole.

2. Next, take the end part of the dizi and fix it onto the other end of the dizi's body. You want a snug and secure fit, so it doesn't fall off.

Now, it's time to learn how to correctly attach the dimo to the dizi. This is one skill you'll need to practice getting it right. There are several ways you could do it, but the method you're about to learn is one of the most efficient ways to attach your dizi membrane. You may want to buy a pack of these to easily replace the membrane. Why? Well, one thing about the membrane is if you get it wet where the hole is, your membrane is done for. You'll no longer have the unique tone that the dimo gives to your playing. So, to attach your dimo, you'll need the following:

- Some water
- Glue
- Small scissors
- Your dimo

4. *Now, it's time to learn how to correctly attach the dimo to the dizi. Source: Dbsboy, CC0, via Wikimedia Commons: https://commons.wikimedia.org/wiki/File:Dizi_dimo.jpg*

Steps

1. First, wet the membrane hole, then wipe it until it is clean and dry. Please get every last drop of water off the hole.

2. Grab your tube of dimo and carefully slit it open with your scissors.

3. Hold your membrane up to the light and study it. If you have a good one, you should notice the dimo's natural lines, which should be parallel relative to the dimo's length.

4. Now, you'll need to make your own lines on the membrane. Your lines should be parallel to the lines already on the membrane. Hold the dimo securely with your thumbs so the natural lines face you. In other words, the lines should be vertical. Give the membrane a wiggle as you gently pull it horizontally. Take it easy with this process. You only need 5 seconds of tugging.

5. Set your membrane down. Take your glued piece and dip it into a little bit of water. You don't need too much water for this step.

6. Apply the wet, glued piece around the hole on your dizi where the membrane should go. As you do this, cover every spot around the hole. Also, only let the glue extend past the hole by no more than half an inch. If you sense there's not enough glue, you can always use some more, but add a little bit each time so you don't go overboard.

7. Remember, you must keep the center of the dimo dry. That's the part that will go over the membrane hole. To keep the strip from getting wet, use your pinky finger to clean any of the glue that may be around or inside the membrane hole. Twirl your finger around so you get every bit of glue that may already be on the inner edge of the membrane hole.

8. Now, it's time to affix the membrane to the membrane hole. Use your thumb to hold one side of the dimo securely against the side of the membrane hole. Then, in one clean move, stretch the other side of the dimo over the hole as firmly as you can while pressing it down against the dizi. This stretch should be a firm one.

9. Take your wet glue stick once more and give it a rub around the dimo's edges. Doing this step means you don't have to worry about the dimo coming loose. This time, your glue stick shouldn't be as wet as the last time you used it, so it will be stickier and give your dimo a firmer hold on your dizi. Remember to keep the center of the membrane dry.

10. Play the dizi and pay attention to how it sounds. If you get a sense that the dimo is too tightly stretched across the membrane hole, you can give it a gentle press as you blow into the instrument. If you press it while not playing it, you'll notice the membrane doesn't loosen up easily. If you find it's too loose, carefully wet the edges of the membrane while avoiding the center, and give the membrane a gentle stretch with your thumbs.

One thing you should know about fixing your dimo to your dizi is that you may need several tries to get it right. So, you should have a few of them handy. Remember, you should never beat yourself up for getting something wrong. You'll need practice, but eventually, you can attach the membrane without much thought or stress.

Choosing the Right Dizi for You

There are many kinds of dizis you could get, but since you're starting out, it's best to look for one that does it all. For starters, you want an instrument that sounds good when you play it. As your playing improves, you may look for something more specific. The following are notes to keep in mind when choosing the best one for you:

1. Pay attention to the intonation of the dizi.

2. If you want the best tone, choose an instrument crafted from dense bamboo.

3. You want a dizi that has a neutral tonal color or quality. The tonal quality makes it possible to tell the difference between two different instruments or voices, even when they're playing or singing the same note.

4. Look for a dizi that feels comfortable as you play it.

Now, you may not be so fortunate as to have a store near you that's stocked with different dizis for you to compare. In that case, you can check out online stores and reviews. You can expect the dizi's quality to be directly correlated to its price tag. In other words, the pricier it is, the better it is. If a dizi is smaller or larger than the standard size, you can also expect it to cost a little more. It's not easy to find high-density bamboo with an even distribution for the smaller dizis, and it's also difficult to find bamboo large enough with a suitable distribution.

Timbre matters a great deal when you're choosing your dizi. Here's a further explanation of this concept. Picture yourself at a concert where various instruments are being played. There are guitars, drums, violins, and pianos. You already know the timbre is why you can tell them apart, but here's how that works. Every sound in music has a single pitch or fundamental note, but other pitches are also present that flavor the main one, thanks to the distinct ways the instruments vibrate as they're played. This is how timbre works. Now, what does this have to do with the dizi you chose? It's an open-pipe instrument, which means it sounds like a brighter concert flute with more buzz, thanks to the extra "flavoring" the dimo gives the dizi's sounds.

There are three basic styles of dizi playing:

- The northern style (or Beipai).

- The southern style (or Nanpai).

- The new style (or Xinpai).

The Beipai style has strong, brilliant notes that are piercing. Playing this way involves a lot of high notes, and you'll have to use techniques like flutter tonguing and double tonguing, among others. So, if you're playing with this style, you'll need a dizi that's responsive and can hit the high notes without sounding like a dying cat. The best dizi for playing Beipai musical pieces is called a bangdi. It has six holes and uses F, G, or A as its base note – so basically, it comes in 3 different versions.

If you're playing Nanpai pieces, play more rounded notes. Unlike the Beipai playing style, you don't have high notes. Rather than playing staccato, the notes flow more in the legato style. You'll also notice the legato notes are sometimes punctuated with shorter ones, with runs of sixteenth notes. So, the best dizi to use for this style of playing is the qudi, which has C or D as its base note (again, it comes in 3 different versions). Like the bangdi, it also has six holes.

How about the Xinpai style? This style is modern, caring less for the distinctions between north and south, which are only relevant when playing classical Chinese folk pieces anyway. Musicians found the distinctions in style an unnecessary limit, so they came up with the Xinpai style of playing. They recognize that the dizi is an instrument far more capable than the rigidities that the previous style would allow. So, Xinpai is a marriage of Beipai and Nanpai, as well as other techniques that were never part of the two earlier ones. The base key of the Xinpai dizi is typically E.

So, when you choose your dizi, you know you have a good one with a neutral tone when the high notes aren't too sharp or shrill, and the lower notes aren't too deep or mellow. Look for one that has brilliant high notes and rounded low ones. It will sound like an excellent middle point between the bangdi and the quidi. When using this dizi, you must put in more work to play a piece for a Beipai or a Nanpai, but that's to be expected. The information in this book will focus on the xiaodi, which also comes in 3 versions depending on its base note, either Bb, C, or D.

The final thing to concern yourself with is how comfortably you can play the dizi. Test it to see how it responds when you blow lightly across the mouth hole. If it's a good one, you'll notice the tone right away, and the pitch will be perfect. Also, it shouldn't feel like you're straining while playing and holding a moderately loud note. If you have to strain, that's no good because when you need to play louder notes for more color, you'll have an even more challenging time.

Also, think about the dizi's weight distribution. When the dizi is in the correct playing position, the weight should feel balanced between your thumbs. If you notice the dizi isn't balanced or is top-heavy, then playing will be a problem because the instrument will keep sliding off your bottom lip. Sure, you could adjust your left hand as you play, but you can't always pull that off. So, choose one that sits right in your hands as you play.

Caring for Your Dizi

1. When you're not playing your dizi, please keep it in its case.

2. Be careful when you handle the dizi. You don't want to drop it or hit it against hard surfaces.

3. Moisture will ruin your dizi, so once you're done playing, wipe it clean on the inside and outside in order to remove the condensation.

4. Don't place your dizi directly in the sun, and don't expose it to cold either, so it doesn't warp or crack.

5. Proactively check your dizi to see if you need to replace the dimo or if it's starting to get worn out so you can make replacements.

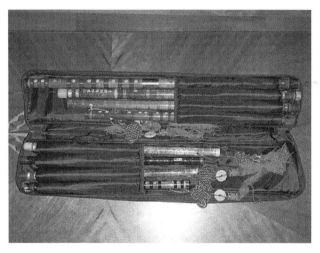

5. When you're not playing your dizi, keep it in its case. Source: David290, CC BY-SA 3.0 <https://creativecommons.org/licenses/by-sa/3.0>, via Wikimedia Commons: https://commons.wikimedia.org/wiki/File:Bag_of_Dizi.jpg

You now know all you need to get started with your dizi. You know its parts as intricately as you know the back of your hand. If you followed the steps correctly, you're now a pro at assembling your instrument. You know the best dizi to pick and how to take care of it. How about getting on to the fun stuff? Find out what that is in the next chapter.

Chapter 3: Learning Dizi Fingerings and Techniques

This is the chapter with everything you've been waiting for. You'll learn how to use your fingers to work some dizi magic. How do you know which hole is which? Which finger goes where? How can you get good at switching your fingers around accurately? You need to know these things to finally create sweet melodies with this ancient, extraordinary instrument. Before talking about your fingers, here's a quick look at what to do with your body. Knowing how to position your fingers won't do you much good if you're not in a comfortable position where you can hold them long enough to play a piece.

What to Do with Your Body

Posture is everything when playing the dizi. You may sit or stand to play as long as you're not uncomfortable and keep your spine neutral. What does that mean? Your spine has natural curves in your neck, middle, and lower areas. So, when it's neutral, that implies your body can move freely and naturally and that you can play your dizi as long as you'd like without straining your muscles, ligaments, and tendons too much. You should also have your head facing forward, whether you are playing by reading sheet music or not.

6. *Posture is everything when playing the dizi. Source: World Intellectual Property Organization, CC BY 2.0 <https://creativecommons.org/licenses/by/2.0>, via Wikimedia Commons: https://commons.wikimedia.org/wiki/File:China_%E2%80%93_A _Celebration_of_the_50th_Anniversary_of_China- WIPO_Cooperation_(53027788084).jpg*

If you have a tilt in your head, you may partially block the airstream from your lips into your dizi. Note that your body will likely tilt to the left when you're holding your dizi in the correct position, which is to your right. It would be best to set up your chair to face the right to keep your head from angling itself when you sit and play. That way, your eyes are straight ahead in front of you. This is a better adjustment than pulling your right arm into your side to accommodate your body's tendency to twist left.

Your upper limbs should be loose and relaxed. Check your shoulders. If you notice any tension in them, relax them. Let them sink down, along with your elbows, to a natural position. You'll know you're doing this right if you feel comfortable and your arms don't extend more than 45 degrees to the right of your body.

What to Do with Your Fingers

There are two things you should remember when fingering your dizi. The first thing is this: keep them ergonomic. Your hands are different from other dizi players, so you have no choice but to adjust the fundamental finger holds so they work for you. Having said that, you will want to hold your dizi correctly so that it sits balanced in your hands. Not only that, but proper finger posture ensures you won't have to stretch your fingers more than necessary, if at all. That's what ergonomics is about.

The second thing to remember is you should keep your fingers loose. You don't have to press down on the holes because you're worried about air escaping. Use no more force than necessary to keep them covered. Why shouldn't you press too hard? If you do, you'll make it tougher to switch from one finger position to another, and that will slow your playing down unpleasantly. When you have to keep one or more holes open, be mindful of how far away your fingers are from them. You shouldn't have them any further than 10 millimeters away from their assigned holes. If they're further than that, it's tough to cover the holes when it's time to play the notes that require them to be covered. If they're too close, you will play a flat version of the note. The best thing to do when it comes to perfect finger ergonomics, and looseness is to keep your knuckles bent so they don't lock. Think of forming the letter "C" with your fingers. That's how you should hold your dizi.

The following are the finger assignments of the dizi's holes:

- Hole 1, right ring finger.
- Hole 2, right middle finger.
- Hole 3, right index finger.
- Hole 4, left ring finger.
- Hole 5, left middle finger.
- Hole 6, left index finger.

Note that hole 1 is the hole at the bottom of the dizi, while hole 6 is closest to the mouthpiece. Your left thumb can either be a little bit off the left to act as a support for your dizi, or it can be right under the left index finger. If you are one of those lucky people with extremely flexible thumbs, you can keep the left thumb sideways and see how you like it. However, never allow your left thumb to stretch past the other fingers on your left hand, nor should you let it move toward your middle finger.

As for your right thumb, it goes beneath the right index finger. If you wish, you can move it slightly to the left so it supports your instrument. Check to ensure you don't have that thumb so far that it stretches into the space your left hand is covering. Also, don't let it stretch beyond your right hand or bend toward your right middle finger.

Your left pinky finger can either rest lightly against the dizi's body, or you can allow it to hang freely. It comes down to the grip you've chosen. As for your right pinky, let it sit on top of your dizi wherever it feels natural. It's okay to allow the right pinky to move with your right ring finger, but only as needed. For instance, if you're playing a trill, you may find it best to allow the right pinky to have some movement. Since you're playing the xioadi dizi, the tone holes are packed tightly together. If you're facing challenges while playing the holes because of how close they are, check to be sure you're only covering them with your fingertips. Sometimes, you'll only need to cover half of a hole. In this case, adjust your fingertips by bringing them closer to your palm.

Basic Fingering Patterns

To keep things simple, there are 7 finger arrangements to concern yourself with when playing your dizi. Using the scale in solfege and playing from the lowest to the highest note, the notes are So, La, Ti, Do, Re, Mi, Fa. If you want to represent this with numbers, write it this way: 5, 6, 7, 1, 2, 3, 4. Classically, the notation begins from Do and ends with Ti before the higher octave, Do, is played, but with the dizi, the starting note is So. So is the fifth note in solfege, and that's why the numbering begins at 5. With that out of the way, here are the fingering patterns you should know:

1. So is the lowest note. It is played with all the holes covered.

2. La is the next note, covering all holes except the lowest one.

3. Ti is the third note. To play, cover all holes except the last two at the bottom.

4. Do, the fourth note, is played with all holes, but the bottom three are closed.

5. The fifth note, Re, is played with all holes, but the lowest four are covered.

6. The sixth note on your dizi is Mi. You cover all holes except for the lowest five to produce this tone.

7. The seventh note, Fa, is a tricky one. You'd think you should open all six holes to play it, but that's not true. Not only is the dizi likely to fall out of your hand if you do that, but you'll also be playing too sharp of a note. So, to play this seventh note, keep the finger hole closest to your mouth open while covering the next two holes after that one. If you do this right, the instrument should be supported by your left ring and middle fingers, as well as your thumb.

Your dizi will likely be pitched to the C or D note in basic staff notation. If you want to know for sure, you can use an app to help you detect the lowest note of your instrument or check out free videos on YouTube with recordings of the note so you can compare by ear.

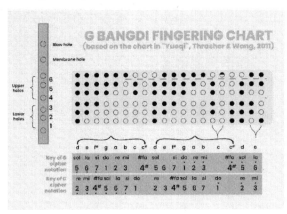

7. Your dizi will likely be pitched to the C or D note in basic staff notation. Source: https://i.pinimg.com/736x/95/c2/55/95c25586ddf9bc7dbc8effd1ecf a464b.jpg

Tips for Developing Finger Agility and Precision

If you want to play the dizi well, work on your fingers. Here's what you can do to help your fingers fly fast from one finger position to the next and cover the holes correctly each time.

1. Always use warm-up exercises before you play. By warming up, you get the blood flowing through your fingers, allowing them to become more flexible. You could warm up by stretching your fingers and clenching them into a fist using slow, deliberate movements.

2. Play scales to get better. Playing the entire scale on the dizi repeatedly for a few minutes is also a good way to fire up those finger muscles. You should start with a simple one first to get your fingers acquainted with the instrument. Start slow. Why? You should be concentrating on playing each note so it rings clearly, and doing that means you have to cover the holes precisely and blow the right amount of air. When you get used to this, you may go faster.

3. Focus on getting stronger, more independent fingers. You need strong fingers to switch from position to position for a long while without feeling tired. There's only one way to accomplish this: through practice. Also, you will have an easier time as you play if you train your fingers to move independently of each other. How can you develop finger strength and independence in one go? You achieve these goals by lifting your fingers one after another while the others remain on the finger holes. You should also press a finger on a hole while the others remain lifted. Practice

this daily, and you'll notice improved dexterity, which means your music will flow smoothly.

4. Use trills. You play trills by switching back and forth between two notes that are adjacent to each other. As always, start slow so you don't get frustrated because you're not hitting the notes correctly. When you feel comfortable, pick up the pace. The more you practice trills, the better and faster your fingers will move.

5. Notice what needs work. When you play, you may notice you have trouble with specific note switches. In that case, you should take extra time to practice them in order to improve.

When you play the dizi, you need your fingers to be in top form. Do you want to play with precision? Would you like to switch seamlessly from note to note? Then, don't ignore the powerful tips you've been given here. Put them to work, and with time, you'll be glad you did. It's the little things like this that move you from the realm of the amateur to being a professional.

Chapter 4: Understanding Dizi Embouchure and Breath Control

It's time to learn what to do with your mouth and how to breathe correctly. You may have assumed there isn't much to learn regarding your lips, lungs, and the dizi, but that's far from the case, as you'll soon discover.

8. *It's time to learn what to do with your mouth and how to breathe correctly. Source: Alex Stoll / Flickr user: N22YF (https://www.flickr.com/photos/n22yf/), CC BY-SA 2.0 <https://creativecommons.org/licenses/by-sa/2.0>, via Wikimedia Commons: https://commons.wikimedia.org/wiki/File:Diziplayer.jpg*

Proper Embouchure Technique

What should you do with your jaw? What about your lips and tongue? These things can affect the sound your dizi makes when you play. First things first, your lips need to be shaped correctly when you play. Traditionally, you're required to shape your lips symmetrically as you play the dizi. However, this is unimportant because not everyone has perfectly balanced lip muscles. So, don't worry if your upper lip has a curve or a dip close to or right in the middle. It doesn't matter because you can adjust both lips as needed. Your embouchure technique involves two things:

- External buccal control.
- Internal buccal control.

Buccal control is a fancy term that explains how you work the muscles of your mouth, including your tongue, cheeks, and lips. So, external buccal control concerns the shape of your lips and how you set your jaw as you play the dizi. If your lips aren't correctly positioned over the mouth hole, you can't play. Your jaw also matters when you play because if you want to create quieter sounds with the dizi, you need to relax it. If you want to hit louder notes, then you need more tension. Also, keep your jaw loose when you want to play softly, but tighten it up if you want to be loud. Your lower lip should cover the embouchure hole by a quarter or a third of the hole. When you rotate the dizi more toward the inside, your playing will sound flatter. Move it outward if you want sharper sounds.

Internal buccal control involves working with your tongue and the shape of your mouth on the inside. Your mouth cavity should be as open and relaxed as possible, almost like you're yawning, but your lips are shut. If it helps, think of the shape your mouth would have if you were about to make a "ha" sound. When you play with this buccal shape, the dizi will play clearly unless you have no mokong for some reason or have too tight of a dimo. In this case, what do you do? You listen to your dizi. Here's how:

1. Cover every finger hole.

2. Put the embouchure or mouth hole near your ear.

3. Pay attention to the echo you can hear within the dizi. What vowel does it sound like? Now, you can set your buccal or mouth cavity as if trying to create that sound when you play.

Now, it's time to talk about your tongue. Where should it go? Your tongue is either resting or moving. When it's at rest as you play the dizi, it's usually because you're playing a long, uninterrupted note, as in a smooth legato. When it's moving, you're articulating and using specific playing techniques like the staccato, for instance. Playing higher notes means you'll need your tongue closer to the front of your mouth, while lower notes require pulling your tongue back.

Breath Control and Steady Airflow

If you want your playing to sound powerful and moving, you need proper breath control and steady airflow. The secret sauce to accomplishing both is knowing how to control your diaphragm. It all begins with breathing. You're playing a wind instrument, so there's no way around breathing. When you play, you should take deep breaths. Allow your belly to balloon as your diaphragm grows flatter, and increase your lung capacity. You don't have to think too deeply to breathe deeply. Imagine filling your belly with air, and your notes will sound smooth and last longer.

What about shallow breathing? Unless you meditate constantly and practice deep breathing, the odds are you are breathing shallow right now. Shallow breathing is normal, everyday breathing for regular people. However, when you practice deep breathing, some pieces will require shallow breathing as you play because there will be snappy notes in them. However, learning to breathe deeply means you can handle any piece that comes your way and keep the airflow steady.

Another interesting breathing technique in order to achieve steady airflow is circular breathing. This method will allow you to keep playing the dizi without having to stop to breathe. If it sounds like there's no way to pull this off without getting dizzy, pun very much intended, that's understandable. The trick to circular breathing is to store some air in your mouth while you blow into your dizi and then, as quickly as you can, inhale through your nose. While doing this, you have to balance the movement of air from your lungs out to your cheeks and from your nose into your lungs. You will definitely need time to get this right, but when you do, it's a trick that will enhance your dizi playing greatly.

If you want to develop breath control, do this simple exercise: Play a tone and continue to exhale for 8 seconds. As you do this, ensure the volume of the note doesn't fluctuate. Practicing this consistently will lead to observable improvements in your playing.

Dynamics and Tone Color

If you want to sound like you were born playing the dizi, play around with tone, color, and dynamics. First, what does tone color even mean? You already know. It's the same thing as timbre. Tone color refers to the overtones you can pick up on, along with the major note played. As you play your dizi, you'll notice these overtones or harmonics. When you're playing notes in the low register, the harmonics are stronger than the main sound. Move up to the middle register of notes, and you'll find a balance between the main sound of those notes and the harmonics. Go to the high register, and the harmonics are weaker than the main sounds. The way to color your playing is through proper buccal control. Play around with various vowel sounds other than the "ha" or "ah" sound. Notice what happens when you use an "ee" or "oh" sound, for instance. You'll realize there are subtle yet powerful differences between the sounds on the same notes. This is how you color your playing.

Another thing you should experiment with is the shape of your lips. Change them as you play, and you'll be astounded by the differences. The rounder your lips are, the purer and more resonant the note will be. If you shape your lips more like an ellipse, you'll add more overtones or harmonics to the note you're playing.

How else can you color your playing? Change the angle of the airflow from your mouth into the dizi, and play around with the speed at which you let the air through. If you blow at a steep angle, you'll cause more pressure in the airflow, and the result will be richer harmonics. If you want to create a piercing shrieking sound, keep your upper lip stiff in order to push the airflow to the downside. If you want a clear sound, relax your upper lip.

Tone color is connected to dynamics, too. If you want to make a portion of your musical piece sound more brilliant because it's soft, or if you want to stop playing shrilly when the music demands loudness, the tone coloring techniques you've just learned about will help you achieve your goal. Note that your ears may pick up on something else compared to what your listeners can hear. It's the same thing when you listen to someone singing up close and personal versus when they're performing on stage and sound even more brilliant. Your dizi's tone color will also depend on the size of the room and the spot you're playing in. So, you should check in with someone knowledgeable and ask about your tone color to see if you need to adjust it.

Now you know what to do with your mouth on the inside and the outside. You've become a master of breath control, playing around with the airflow through your lips and into your dizi like the not-too-distant cousin of the Last Airbender. What's the point of this chapter? If you're tempted to think none of this matters, always remember this: you can't play your dizi if you don't control your breath, and the people listening to you can hear you better when your main sound comes with harmonics or overtones. If the harmonics or overtones are absent, then your sound won't be projected as you'd like, and the audience may not enjoy your playing.

Chapter 5: Playing Your First Note and Simple Melodies

You know how to work your fingers and lungs, and you've picked up a few nifty tricks to go from basic blowing to artistic expression with your dizi. There's no reason to put this off any longer. It's about time you learned to play simple melodies. You could always play songs by ear, but in this chapter, you'll also learn how to read basic dizi notation and keep time. Knowing how to read music will open up a world full of millions of tunes you can enjoy and play in addition to the songs you've already heard. How cool is that?

Reading Basic Dizi Notation and Rhythm

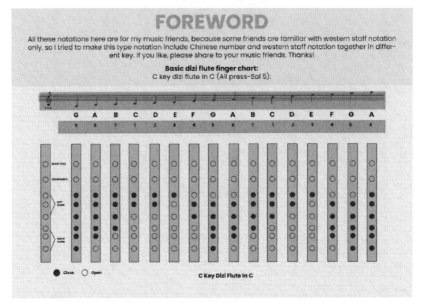

9. *Knowing how to read music will open up a world full of millions of tunes you can enjoy and play in addition to the songs you've already heard. Source: https://custom-images.strikinglycdn.com/res/hrscywv4p/image/upload/c_limit,fl _lossy,h_1000,w_500,f_auto,q_auto/3654546/172594_446047.pn g*

The Chinese have a numbered musical notation method, known as jianpu, typically used with other Chinese instruments, including the dizi. These are the basic principles you need to understand about the jianpu:

1. **The Numbers:** The numbers in the jianpu go from 1 to 7. If you're wondering if they share a connection with the 7 notes of a musical scale, you'd be right. When playing in the key of C major, you'd be playing these notes, matched to their corresponding letters:

   a. 1 represents C.

---

b. 2 represents D.

c. 3 represents E.

d. 4 represents F.

e. 5 represents G.

f. 6 represents A.

g. 7 represents B.

2. **The Dots:** When reading jianpu notation, you'll notice that some numbers have dots. When they're on top of the numbers, these dots mean you need to play the note on a higher octave. If you find the dot below a number, you will play that note on a lower octave. So, finding an upper-dotted 2 when the musical piece is in the key of D major would mean you're to play the next higher version of the E note. What if you notice there are two dots above a number? In that case, you should play the note two octaves higher. The same logic applies regardless of the number of dots or where these multiple dots occur on a number.

3. **The Lines:** Some numbers in jianpu have a line beneath them. The line tells you to play the note half as long as you would a regular one. So, when there's only a number on the jianpu, play it for one beat in a musical bar or as long as a crotchet would last. Note that a crotchet is the same as a quarter note, and four quarter notes would make up a bar of music played in 4/4 time. So, the following are the interpretations of lines below numbers in jianpu:

   a. No line: Play a crochet or quarter note.

   b. 1 line: Play a quaver or an eighth note.

   c. 2 lines: Play a semiquaver or a sixteenth note.

d. 3 lines: Play a demisemiquaver or a thirty-second note. Fun fact: there is also the hemidemisemiquaver, the semihemidemisemiquaver, the demisemihemidemisemiquaver, and... well, you can go on from there. Typically, it's not expected to have to play notes of these durations.

4. **The Dashes**: Sometimes, a note has to be played longer than its standard duration. To represent this extension, a dash comes after the number in jianpu. When this happens, you're expected to play the beat longer by one crotchet. So, when you're playing in C major, and you see 1 - - -, that implies you're meant to play the C key and let it ring for three more crotchet beats. Add the first beat in which you played the note, and you'll have four crotchets (or a semibreve), also known as a whole note.

5. **The Score**: You'll find the score for the musical piece you're playing at the top left of the jianpu sheet. Those numbers tell you how many beats should be played in a bar. This part tells you the rhythm of the piece you're playing. So, a piece with three beats in a bar would be written as 3/4, while one with 4 beats in a bar would be 4/4.

A Note on Scales

Like any other musical instrument, the dizi is played in various keys. For instance, if you're playing a dizi with its base note as the D key, you would be playing D, E, F# (F sharp), G, A, B, C# (C sharp), and D on the next octave. However, when you play a different scale, like G major, on this same dizi, your fingering would have to change. Remember that with jianpu notation, the scale can move around. In other words, the number 1 doesn't have to be a C. It could be a G or a D, depending on the scale the musical piece is to be played in.

As long as you have the thumb hole and the holes of your left hand closed on the dizi, you have the note that acts as the basic or foundational note. If you're meant to play a song in a specific key, the notation on the musical sheet will indicate it. For instance, the notation could say 1 = D. In that case, you need a dizi with the D note as its base. If it says 1 = G, you need a dizi with the G as the root note. When you're playing solo pieces, you can use any dizi to play those scales.

Playing Beginner-Friendly Melodies to Gain Confidence

Now that you know how to read the jianpu, you should begin your dizi journey by learning simple melodies. The best ones are beginner-friendly and uncomplicated. At first, you may think that's not exciting, but here's the thing: You should start slow and simple in order to build confidence in your ability to play. Search for melodies that only have basic rhythms and notes. As you play them consistently, you'll make progress quickly.

If you don't want to use musical sheets, you can play your favorite tunes by ear. Choosing the songs you already know and love is the smart way to get hooked on playing the dizi because you'll be excited to learn them. It also doesn't hurt that the people in your life are more likely to be familiar with those tunes and less likely to bite your head off as you practice because they can follow your progress and feel like they're part of your journey. You'll also get feedback from them, which will let you know how you've been doing.

Simpler melodies are great for training your ears, too. Most people enjoy music, but not everyone has a musically-trained ear. As you learn the simple songs before moving on to more complicated ones, you'll gain an understanding and appreciation of rhythm, melody, and pitch. These elements are essential to your development as a musician, particularly as a dizi player. So, start off with familiar and simple tunes that only require basic finger positions, go slow, and then build your practice from there. If you want to make the process even more enjoyable, you can get backing tracks to the songs. These tracks are excellent for staying in rhythm and watching your timing as you play. Remember all the tips you were given in the previous chapter on how to play precise and steady sounds on the dizi, and you'll be fine.

So, you know how to read dizi notation like you have Chinese blood flowing through your veins, and you know the essence of starting with simple songs to get better at playing. What else is next? Find out in the next chapter.

Chapter 6: Exploring Different Techniques

You've had some practice with your favorite songs, and now your heart is ready for something more. This chapter will feed that hunger. What do you think about mastering powerful techniques to play music on the dizi? You're going to learn about these powerful playing methods in this chapter.

Breath Techniques

You can make your playing more interesting by using breathing techniques. Here's a look at some cool things you can do with your breath.

Pauses: In jianpu, you may see a little "v" in between the notes. When you do, you're meant to take a breath with your mouth quickly. You may use your nose to inhale, but only if that's the end of a portion of the musical piece. It's better to use your mouth if it's a pause meant to help you keep up with the speed of a musical piece.

Tenuto: This technique is also called baochiyin. You're meant to play the note and hold it. With this method, you're not allowed to drop the strength of your breath from the start to the finish of the note. In jianpu, you'll see the tenuto mark as a little dash that goes on top of the notes you should play this way.

Accent: Also called qiangyin, this technique requires you to attack the note powerfully. So, at the start of the note, your breath will be heavy and short, and then you allow it to quickly drop off in intensity. You know the feeling when you're starting to sneeze? That's how you should play when you come across accented notes. Notes to be played this way have the "greater than" symbol (or ">") above them.

Flutter Tongue: The flutter tongue technique is also called huashe. The way it works is you take the note and break it into shorter bits. For this, you will need to use your tongue. So, why is this a breath technique? The only way to pull this off is while you're exhaling. Any note that has an asterisk sign above it in jianpu is a note to be played this way. To pull this technique off, keep the following in mind:

1. Your tongue should flutter through the air you expel from your lungs into the dizi.

2. Brace both sides of your tongue by gently curving them into your soft palate. If you do this right, the tip of your tongue will be free. You should place the tip behind your upper front teeth.

3. You need to practice getting the feel of how much air you need to pass through your tongue and channel across the tongue's tip to help it flutter.

Uvular trill: This method also involves fluttering. It's called the houyin. The difference between this and the huashe is you move your throat while exhaling as if you're trying to clear it and repeat that motion.

Dynamics Techniques

Dynamics refers to how loud or soft the tone you're playing is. The symbols for the different techniques you will learn in jianpu notation are the same as those in Western notation, and they will go below the notes they affect.

Word	Common Abbreviation	English Definition and Description	Symbol
Crescendo	Cresc.	Growing louder. Symbol indicates the magnitude of the increase in volume	p ◁ mf
Decrescendo	Decresc.	Growing softer. Symbol indicates the magnitude of the decrease in volume	f ▷ p
Diminuendo	Dim.	Another term for decrescendo	
Forte	f	Loud	
Fortepiano	fp	Loud then immediately soft	
Fortissimo	ff or fff	Very loud or very very loud	
Mezzo forte	mf	Moderately loud	
Mezzo piano	mp	Moderately soft	
Piano	p	Soft. Gentle	
Pianissimo	pp or ppp	Very soft or very very soft. Almost gives the feeling like you are whispering	

10. *Dynamics refers to how loud or soft the tone you're playing is.*
Source: https://cdn-
kjhmj.nitrocdn.com/stfdlijTYHYYmwrXUrvaWHcZEiWqNDpg/ass
ets/images/optimized/rev-e84cc05/www.theflutecoach.com/wp-
content/uploads/2017/10/Dynamics-table.png

Piano, Pianissimo, and Pianississimo: These terms require you to play soft, softer, and even softer, respectively. All you have to do is reduce how much air you expel from your lungs. Note that you'll have to adjust your jaw as you play in order to account for the flatness that happens when you play softly. Shifting your jaw forward causes the note to sound sharper while shifting it backward will flatten it. You only need to move your jaw slightly to achieve the note-bending effect, and if you do it right, you should be able to sharpen or flatten the notes by a semitone or two. Your goal when playing softly is to express different dynamics while maintaining a steady pitch. The symbols for these three dynamics are p, pp, and ppp.

Forte, Fortissimo, Fortississimo: You need to play loud, louder, and even louder. As a result, you'll be pushing more air than needed through the dizi, which means you'll have sharper-sounding notes. By slightly moving your jaw backward, you can correct the sharpness while keeping the loudness. Unlike the softer dynamics, the loud notes may not be sustainable for very long. The symbols are f, ff, and fff.

Crescendo and Diminuendo: Crescendo is a gradual rise in volume, while diminuendo is a gradual drop. So, as you gradually increase the airflow, you need to bend the note so it's flatter. When you gradually decrease the airflow to drop the volume of the note, sharpen the note.

Vibrato: This technique requires you to oscillate your stomach as you exhale, causing the airflow to vary. Think of it like creating a wavy line with the note. As it turns out, in jianpu, the vibrato is represented with a wavy line above the notes that you should play that way.

Tongue Techniques

Articulation is essential when playing the dizi. It's what your tongue does while you play. You'll need to understand how consonants and vowels are important when articulating.

Vowels: First, revisit the matter of buccal shape. You can use the shape of your mouth on the inside to generate various kinds of harmonics. Here are the vowel shapes to remember:

- Fundamental or basic note: [o] as in "oh" in "coal".

- Second harmonic: [u] as in "ooh" in "you".

- Third harmonic: [ə] as in "uh" in "bird" without the "r" sound.

- Fourth harmonic: [y] as in "ü" in the German word "über".

- Fifth harmonic: [i] as in "ee" in "see".

The higher the notes you want to hit, the more closed and forward your tongue becomes while keeping the embouchure open enough to allow a consonant. When the harmonics come closer to the fundamental, your tongue goes further back to create a vowel.

Consonants: Consonants are the attacking and decaying of your musical tone, and they require your tongue to move around. There are two groups of consonants:

- The shejian consonant with the tongue tip.

- The shegen consonant with the base of the tongue.

With the shejian, you have three possible positions to place your tongue in. These are the key sounds for the tongue positions:

- "T" or [t] for hard articulation on higher notes.

- "D" or [d] for single tonguing and softer articulation on lower notes.

- "R" or [ɹ] for flutter tonguing.

There are three positions for the shegen:

- "K" or [kh].

- "G" or [g] for double tonguing.

- "R" or [r] for uvular flutter tonguing.

Note that the [kh] and [g] sounds are good for double-tonguing.

Now that you know all this, here's a quick look at the tongue articulations you can use as you play, with the tempi gradually increasing:

Articulation or Qingtu (D)

- 1st: [doː]
- 2nd: [duː]
- 3rd: [dɵː]
- 4th: [dyː]
- 5th: [diː]

Articulation or Qingtu (DG)

- 1st: [doːgoː]
- 2nd: [duːguː]
- 3rd: [dɵːgɵː]
- 4th: [dyːgyː]
- 5th: [diːgiː]

Staccato or Dantu (T)

- 1st: [to]
- 2nd: [tu]
- 3rd: [tɵ]
- 4th: [ty]
- 5th: [ti]

Staccato or Shuangtu (TK)

- 1st: [tokʰo]
- 2nd: [tukʰu]
- 3rd: [tɵkʰɵ]
- 4th: [tykʰy]
- 5th: [tikʰi]

Staccato or Santu (T TK)

- 1st: [ˈto.tokʰo]
- 2nd: [ˈtu.tukʰu]
- 3rd: [ˈtɵ.tɵkʰɵ]
- 4th: [ˈty.tykʰy]
- 5th: [ˈti.tikʰi]

Staccatissimo or Dantu (T)

- 1st: [tŏ]
- 2nd: [tŭ]
- 3rd: [tɵ̆]
- 4th: [ty̆]
- 5th: [tĭ]

Staccatissimo or Shuangtu(TK)

- 1st: [tŏkʰŏ]
- 2nd: [tŭkʰŭ]
- 3rd: [tɵ̆kʰɵ̆]
- 4th: [ty̆kʰy̆]
- 5th: [tĭkʰĭ]

Flutter Tongue or Huashe

- 1st: [ɻo]
- 2nd: [ɻu]
- 3rd: [ɻɵ]
- 4th: [ɻy]
- 5th: [ɻi]

You now have an arsenal of techniques to elevate your dizi playing skills. These techniques can be used in traditional or modern music, so don't feel like you can only use them in one or the other.

Chapter 7: Adding Expression and Vibrato

Did you know there are even more ways to make your playing more expressive than you've already learned? Even the vibrato can be achieved in multiple ways. It's the little ornamentations you add to your dizi music that give your playing some flair. These skills set you apart from amateurs, and you're about to learn them all, starting now.

More on the Vibrato

You've learned a little about the vibrato, but there's more. Vibrato is fantastic because it makes your music sound deep. It adds warmth to your notes, creating a feeling that tugs on everyone's heartstrings. You're already familiar with using your breath to induce vibrato, but did you know you could use your fingers and wrists, too?

Finger Vibrato: This technique will help your music sound more expressive, and it's not a tough one to pull off. If you find the diaphragm or breathing vibrato challenging, you'll love this one.

1. First, choose a note that you'd like to try this on. You have to sustain the note for longer than usual to pull it off.

2. Next, keep your breath steady, as you can't afford to switch the dynamics or volume while you do this. If you haven't developed breath control yet, you should work on that first before you attempt this technique.

3. Move the finger that is covering the hole of the note you want to play up and down. You don't need to move your finger wildly. Instead, keep control of your finger by using gentle taps on the hole.

4. While you play the finger vibrato, experiment with the speed at which you tap your finger. Go faster, then go slower, and note the differences in vibrato effect. The goal is to learn what speed would work best with a musical piece.

If you want to make people feel deeply as you play and maybe turn every dry eye wet, then you should use this technique. It's best to work it into the phrases of music that are most poignant so the listeners can feel the fire of passion, the depths of longing, the weight of sadness, or whatever it is you want them to feel.

Wrist Vibrato: For the wrist vibrato, all you need to do is rock your wrist back and forth horizontally while playing a long, smooth note. If you can pull this off with consistency and control your movements, you'll notice a more colorful fluctuation in the pitch of your note. As with the finger vibrato and diaphragm vibrato, you should save the wrist version for those dramatic moments in the music you're playing. Also, you have to find the rhythm between your breath control and your wrist movement. Continue to blow steadily, as your wrist does all the vibrato work here, not your lungs.

If you'd like to have a rich and nuanced vibrato, you may combine all three of the different kinds and see how that works. The odds are you will fall in love with this technique, so try not to overdo it.

Ornamentation Techniques

Grace Notes: These notes are short and quick. They're decorative or ornamental notes you use to embellish your music. You play them right before the main note you're about to play in the piece in order to give the music more color. When you practice a melody, see if you can play a quick note before a main one. You'll know you've got it right when the timing and rhythm of your music aren't thrown off, and the grace note matches the melody.

Trills: When you play trills with your dizi, you rapidly move your finger off and on a hole. Grace notes are meant to be played rapidly and once, but trills last long, which means they're excellent for ornamenting the more extended notes in your music.

Slides and Glissandos: When you play a slide on your dizi, you move gradually from one note to the next rather than abruptly. That's why this technique is called a "slide." How do you pull it off? By gradually covering or uncovering the holes, you cause this gradual shift in pitch. You could play an ascending slide with a note that gradually goes up the music scale to a higher one or a descending slide that gradually drops down the scale. The glissando is a specific kind of slide that requires playing with more than two notes, and it's a lot faster than a regular slide. The notes in a glissando are meant to be played quickly, one after another, and if you use this technique, you'll achieve some dramatic effects in your music.

If you've been following so far, the odds are you understand you'll need to work on your embouchure to help you pull off the note bending.

Emphasizing Dynamics, Phrasing, and Musicality

In the previous chapter, you learned about the different dynamic techniques you can use to give your music more nuance as you play. So, when you practice, the more you play with dynamics and ornamentation, the more skillful and enjoyable your dizi playing will sound. In other words, the variations in loudness and softness, along with the other embellishments, will create musicality as you play, taking ordinary notes and transforming them into a true melody that tells a story.

Phrasing is the structure of the notes you're playing... it's how all those notes come together to give your music depth and meaning that your listeners can relate to. Think of it like creating sentences in a language. These sentences, put together, will create meaning or a story. However, they have to be in the correct order and flow well together. Why? If you don't arrange the words properly, then readers might either lose sight of whatever message you want to convey, or they'll get the message, but you won't keep their attention. Phrasing also matters in music. It involves articulation, which you've already learned in the previous chapter. It's also about how the dynamics, musical structure, breath, punctuation, and rhythms are put together in an artistic manner that is uniquely yours. These are the elements you must master to create your personal style as you play. When you become proficient with these techniques, your music will naturally be full of emotion.

At this point, no one will ask you to keep your playing down anymore. They want to hear you play because each time you do, you get them right in the feels. That's something to aspire to.

Chapter 8: Progressing as a Dizi Player

This is the final chapter of this book, but not the final chapter of your journey with the dizi. You know how to work the different technical aspects of playing this instrument in order to create sweet, magical sounds that pull tears from every eye and soften the hardest of hearts. What now? You have to continue making progress, and you're about to learn how.

Setting Personal Goals

Goals are necessary for tracking your progress with the dizi. If you don't set goals, then how will you know how far you've come or if you are making improvements? Also, when you can see how well you're doing over time, you remain motivated. You'll be inspired to pick up your dizi and play, even after your regular practice time. Here's how to set your goals, track your progress, and smash each target every time.

11. Goals are necessary for tracking your progress with the dizi.
Source: https://pixabay.com/photos/bulletin-board-stickies-post-it-3127287/

1. What are your goals? Define them. Do you want to get better at breath control? Would you like to master the glissando? Do you want to be part of an ensemble? By knowing what your goal is, it becomes immediately apparent when you achieve it.

2. Get specific. When you refine your goals so they're specific, you'll find it easier to accomplish them. Some people keep things too general by saying, "I'd like to become a pro at the dizi." Well, that's not enough. How about, "I'd like to play this song faster and with no mistakes?" That kind of specificity will go a long way toward helping you improve. You have a target, and when you hit the bull's eye, you'll surely know it.

3. Make your goals realistic. If you get too ambitious, you'll feel frustrated, snap your dizi in half, and call it a day. So, don't intend to master a complicated piece in a few minutes or an hour when you know it's unrealistic. Otherwise, you could chunk that goal down. Split it into smaller targets. Could you, perhaps, pick only one section of that complicated piece and give yourself a week to master that before moving on to the next

portion? That would be a more realistic and, therefore, achievable target.

4. Create a schedule and stick to it. The only way to achieve your goals is through practice. You can't just write down some goals and hope that the Law of Attraction or your favorite superhero will magically make them happen without you putting in the work. It doesn't happen that way. So, have a practice schedule and stick to it. You can link it to something you must do every day so you can't get around it.

5. Track your progress. You could record your practice sessions and play them back later, comparing them to previous ones to see how you're doing. Also, use a journal to write down what you're getting better at and what you should tighten up. Make a habit of reviewing your notes.

As you track your progress, take the time to celebrate all your improvements, no matter how small they seem. You deserve to acknowledge your effort, and by celebrating yourself, you're more likely to keep going and setting new goals to smash.

Exploring More Advanced Techniques and Repertoire

At some point, things may feel too easy. When you notice this happening, it's time to take on new challenges. You'll need to work with a dizi teacher who has enough experience in the more complicated techniques so you can make your playing even more nuanced. You'll also have to learn more advanced fingering patterns to allow yourself to play various pieces of music that are far more complicated than anything you've done so far. You may look for resources on the internet to guide you, but at some point, you'll find it helpful to take an actual course or get a dizi master to walk you through the things you don't know.

As you grow more confident in your ability to work the dizi like it's a part of you, you should actively search for more intricate compositions with unique melodies and rich dynamics. This is how you expand your repertoire. Don't shy away from any genre. Take it all on, and you'll notice how they give you bits and pieces that will eventually become part of your style. Working with other musicians is also a good idea for learning what else is new that you haven't already learned. Remember, you made peace with the fact that you'll be a lifelong learner, so don't feel like you're taking many steps back by working with an instructor or more knowledgeable players. Keep an open mind, and you'll be glad you did.

Tips for Continuous Improvement

1. Practice every day. It's better to practice for ten minutes daily than to have one three-hour practice every other week.

2. Always warm up before you play so your fingers, mouth, and lungs are ready.

3. Regardless of how much you improve, continue to work on your finger dexterity by learning how to move them independently of one another.

4. Create a list of musical pieces and learn them in the order of increasing complexity. When you have a list to work with, you stay inspired and driven to continue your dizi practice.

5. Listen to music with the dizi as a prominent feature, whether as a solo instrument or part of an ensemble. Why? You will train your ears to pick up on different things the musicians do with the instrument, and you will find yourself intuitively replicating those techniques.

6. Explore a variety of genres other than Chinese traditional music to understand how the dizi works in other contexts.

7. Play with other musicians. There is no better way to improve than by seeing how you can fit into a musical piece with your dizi. If you can't find others to play with, you should look for backing music.

8. Be patient with yourself. You know the saying: "Rome wasn't built in a day," so don't assume you can be a dizi master in a ridiculously short time. It will take as long as it takes.

9. Your mastery of the instrument will progress faster if you set goals.

10. Teach others. The saying, "Those who can't teach," is false. When you teach, you learn and improve. So, don't shy away from a chance to show others what you've learned.

Conclusion

Learning to play the dizi is an exciting and rewarding thing to do because you're not only mastering this beautiful instrument but discovering a new way to express yourself. Nothing feels better than expressing your emotions through music. Also, it doesn't hurt that it's good for your mental health. By playing the dizi, you provide catharsis for yourself, and the others around you can hear you. However, this catharsis won't happen at the start of your journey, so you have to be patient with yourself. You're going to make mistakes, and there will be times when you feel like there's no point because you're stuck or you've plateaued. However, you have to keep going because by putting one foot in front of the other, you will get a breakthrough and develop more skills than you thought possible.

Remember, all you need are time and consistency with your practice. Make peace with the fact that this is a journey. You can't teleport your way to mastery. If you could, then there would be no point in writing or reading this book, and no one would bother teaching anyone anything. Every skill requires patience and commitment to master. So, enjoy the process. There's no rush. One day, you'll stumble on one of your recordings from the start of your dizi-learning journey, and you'll be in awe over how far you've come. For that day to happen, you only have one thing to do: Play your heart out.

References

Baxter, M. L. (2001). The Chinese dizi, the Native American courting flute, and the Andean panpipes: An investigation of pedagogy and musical practice. Teachers College, Columbia University.

Brookhaven Lab Expert Helps Date Flute Thought To Be Oldest Playable Musical Instrument. (n.d.). ScienceDaily. https://www.sciencedaily.com/releases/1999/10/991005071115.htm

Brooks De Wetter-Smith. (1978). Sound Modification Techniques in Selected Flute Repertoire Since 1966.

Chung, L. C. (2018). Intercultural Musicking: A study of the dizi from a Western flute perspective (Doctoral dissertation).

Lau, F. (2008). Music in China: experiencing music, expressing culture. Oxford University Press.

Lawrence, L. (2021). The Self-Taught Flute Player. Uptake Publications.

Lee, H. H. (2017). How to Play Dizi, the Chinese Bamboo Flute.

Li, M. (1995). Di-zi: the history and performance practice of the Chinese bamboo transverse flute. The Florida State University.

Mu, Y. (1993). Chinese musical instruments: an introduction.

Pellerite, J. (1963). Handbook of Literature for the Flute. Alfred Music.

Raine-Reusch, R. (2010). Play The World: The 101 Instrument Primer. Mel Bay Publications.

Thrasher, A. R. (2023). Traditional Instruments and Heterophonic Practice. The Oxford Handbook of Music in China and the Chinese Diaspora.

Toff, N. (2012). The flute book: a complete guide for students and performers. Oxford University Press.

Made in the USA
Columbia, SC
21 December 2024

50276498R10039